INSTRUCTIONAL GUIDE TO
SURFING

INSTRUCTIONAL GUIDE TO SURFING
QUICK TIPS

Written by Ceasar Cabral
Illustrated by Ron Croci

Published and distributed by

ISLAND HERITAGE
P U B L I S H I N G

99-880 Iwaena Street
Aiea, Hawai'i 96701-3202
Telephone 808-487-7299
Fax 808-488-2279
hawaii4u@islandheritage.com

ISBN 0-89610-109-6
First Edition, First Printing, 2000

INSTRUCTIONAL GUIDE TO
SURFING

QUICK TIPS

By Ceasar Cabral

With Illustrations by Ron Croci

ISLAND HERITAGE

Contents

TO THE SURFER

I congratulate you for taking the first steps
to learning how to surf. The techniques I offer in this guide
will help you increase your chances
of learning to surf safely and well. Surfing has given me
confidence and self-esteem. I hope this book
will help do the same for you.
I have surfed in both the Pacific Islands and
California, and I've experienced both good days and bad days.
It takes a lot of time, practice, and patience
to master the skill of surfing, but eventually it all pays off.
So hang in there!
Like any new exercise plan, if you have any
physical problems, please check with your physician first.
You will be surfing at your own risk. Good luck,
God bless, and have fun!

It is important to learn to surf on a proper-sized surfboard. For example, a person who is 5 feet 5 inches tall, weighing approximately 125 pounds, would require at least a 7 1/2- to 8 1/2-foot-long board. You need as much of the board above water as below to eliminate any water drag. This float will increase your chances of catching a wave.

Surfboard Conditions

Any cracks, chips, or loose fiberglass should be repaired to avoid serious injuries.

Surfboard Body Parts

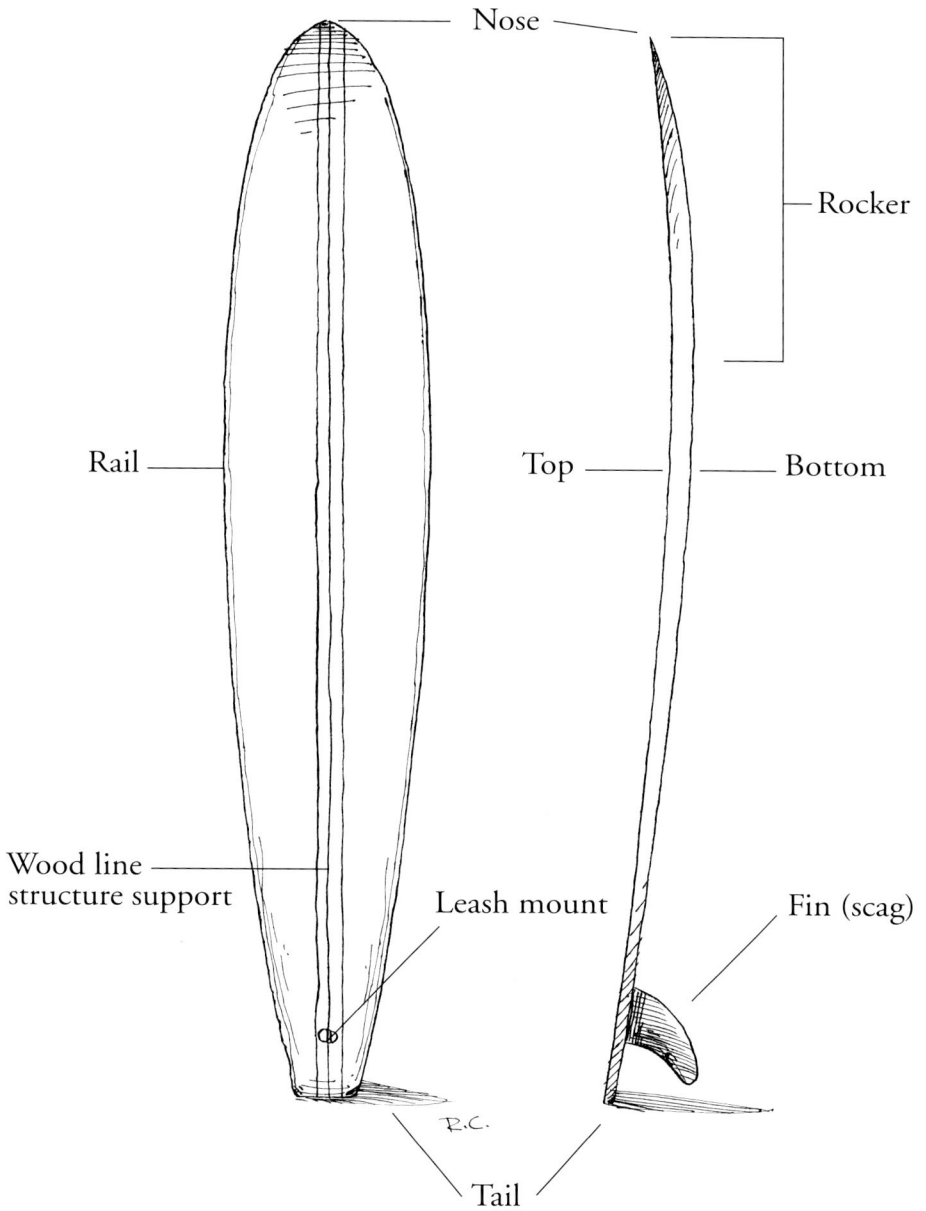

Nose

Rocker

Rail

Top — — Bottom

Wood line
structure support

Leash mount

Fin (scag)

R.C.

Tail

Board Waxing: To Stick, Not Slip

Wax is a must! Rubbing a bar of surf wax on your board in a circular motion, wax only the top of the board from nose to tail, and wax only the top half of the side rails. This will prevent you from slipping off your board when sitting or standing.

Put It on a Leash

Be sure your board is equipped with a leash to strap to your ankle. Chasing a loose board can be frustrating. The leash should be strapped to the ankle of the leg closest to the leash mount when you are standing on the board.

A wet suit should be worn in cold water conditions to avoid muscle fatigue and hypothermia. There are many styles of wet suits to choose from.

Winter Suit

A winter suit keeps you fully covered, while the sleeves and legs of a spring suit are short.

Spring Suit

Stretch

Surfing is a physical sport. Just as any good athlete does before a workout, you should give your muscles a decent stretch to avoid cramping.

Standing Exercises

In addition to the usual stretching exercises, I recommend the following simple floor exercise for standing skill and speed:

Step 1: Position yourself down on the floor in a push-up position.

Step 2: Push your body up in a lunge position.

Step 3: Hop to a standing position with your legs shoulder-length apart as if you were surfing.

Time to Get Wet

Most boards have a wood line running down their center from nose to tail. When lying on your board, use the wood line as a guide to keep your body straight. Your head should be up so you can see where you are going. Keep your legs together and your toes comfortably pointed. The nose of your surfboard should be at least 1 1/2 to 2 1/2 inches out of the water. This will help you slide faster on top of the water.

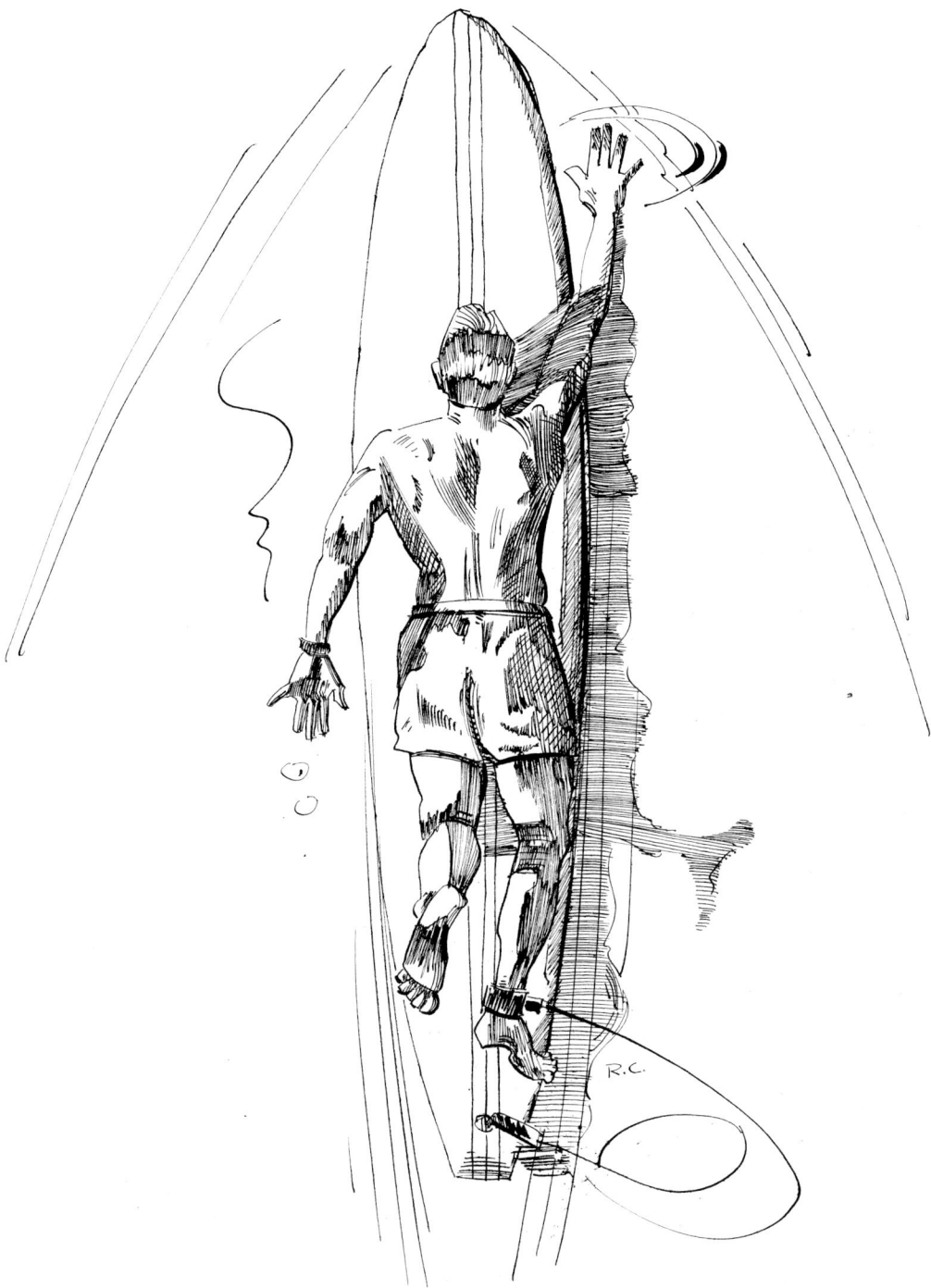

There are several ways to avoid getting pushed back too far by the whitewash as you paddle out toward the waves. The whitewash you will have to get across may be up to 3 to 4 feet high.

Technique 1

At 2 to 5 feet before the whitewash hits you, push the nose of your board down by using a ducking motion, thus diving with your board underneath the whitewash. After coming back up to the surface, start paddling again to get out to the waves.

1. Paddle out to about 2 to 5 feet before the whitewash.

2. Using a ducking motion, push the nose of your board down

3. Dive with your board underneath the whitewash.

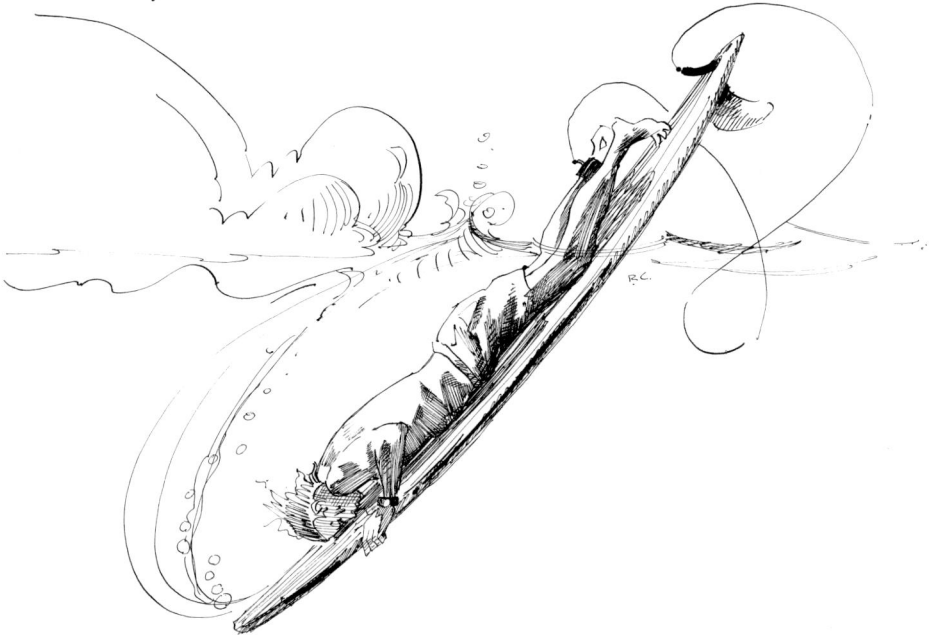

4. Come back up to the surface.

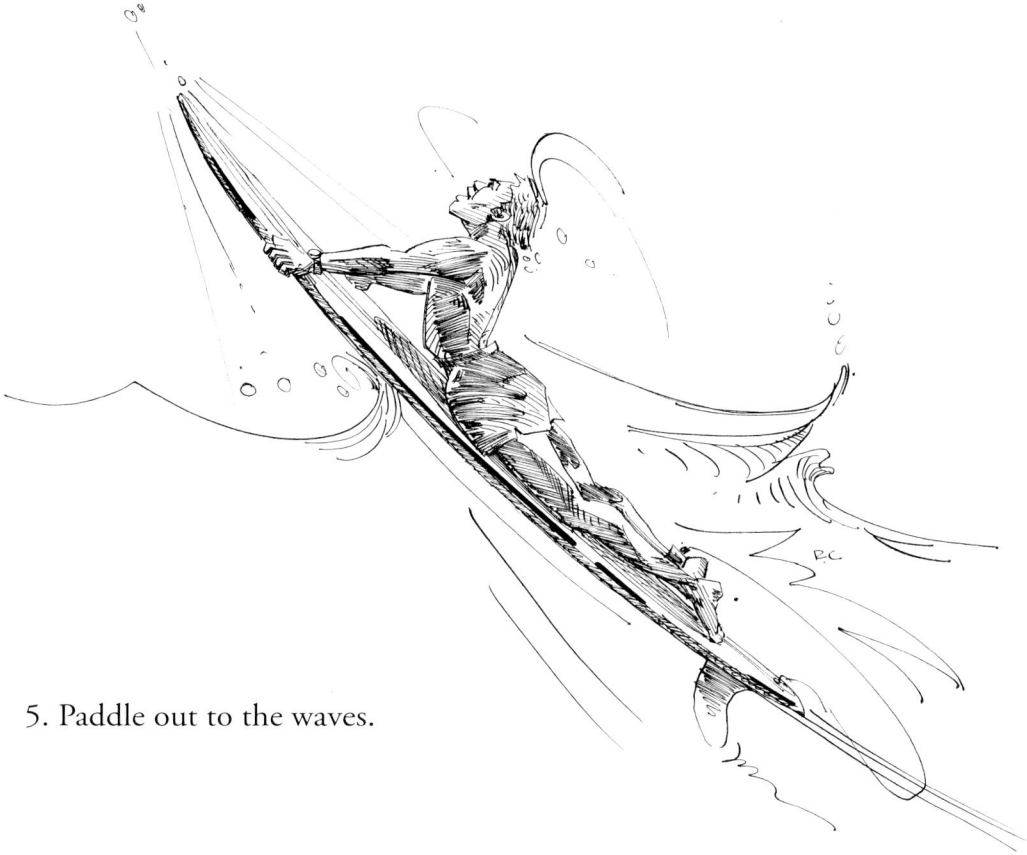

5. Paddle out to the waves.

Technique 2

Paddle out until the whitewash is about 4 to 8 feet in front of you. Using a barrel roll motion, flip your body over with your board. Hold on to the nose of the surfboard firmly and pull down to create a ramp. Allow 3 to 6 seconds for the wave to pass, depending on its size, then roll out and paddle away. With practice you will get the hang of it. Eventually you will develop your own timing.

1. Paddle out to about 4 to 8 feet before the whitewash.

2. Using a barrel roll motion, flip your body over with your board.

3. Hold on to the nose of the surfboard and pull down to create a ramp.

R.C.

4. Allow 3 to 6 seconds
for the wave to pass.

R.C.

5. Remain under your board until the wave passes over.

6. Roll out and get on your board.

7. Paddle out to the waves.

It's time to sit on your board and look like you know what you are doing. The main technique to sitting on your board is to relax your body. Relaxation is essential.

Position yourself slightly behind the center of the board with your legs hung over the sides. Keep the surfboard nose out of the water, unless you are on a long board (see illustration). Your arms should extend in front of you. Hold the side rails of the board for center balance.

To stabilize yourself in the water, first relax your body. Then use a kicking motion, lifting your left leg when rolling to the right. Do the same motion as you are rolling to the left, lifting your right leg. These movements can be practiced with a surfboard in a swimming pool.

1. Sit slightly behind the center of the board with your legs hung over the side

2. Keeping the surfboard nose out of the water, extend your arms and hold the side rails.

3. Rolling to the right, lift your left leg using a kicking motion.

4. Rolling to the left, use a kicking motion to lift your right leg.

5. If you are using a long board (8 1/2 feet or more in length), kneel on the board and keep the nose of the board level with the water. Paddle with your arms to keep your balance.

The Line Up

The line up is where most surfers park themselves to wait for waves.

Use discretion and courtesy.

Toward Shore

Mark It

When you find a good spot where you are catching the waves, remember where you "parked." To do that, use objects to your right, to your left, and in front of you as markers just in case you forget or drift off from where you are catching your waves.

You are here.

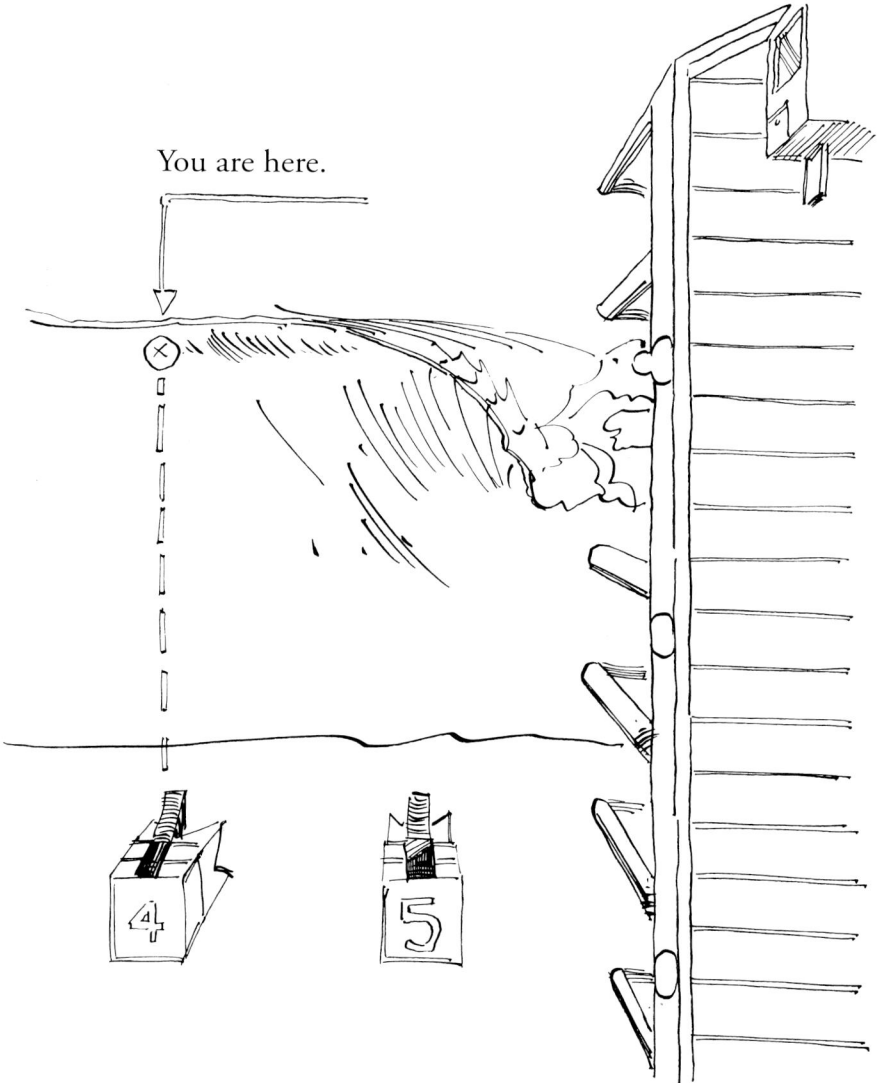

Top View

Caution! Trying to surf waves more than 4 feet high can be hazardous for the beginner. When learning how to surf, it is ideal to start on 2- to 4-foot waves in order to prevent serious injuries to yourself or to others.

Normally there are about two to four waves in a set. If you miss the first wave, turn around and be prepared for the next incoming wave. This alertness will help you throughout the day. Remember to be observant of other surfers.

As a wave approaches at four to five car lengths behind you, start paddling slowly toward the shore. When it is about one car length away, start paddling as hard as you can, glancing back to make sure the wave did not break too soon. As the wave lifts you up, hop up on the board to your stance and prepare for that forward slide. You are now surfing!

1. Sit on your board, both arms extended and holding the side rails.

2. Keep the nose of your board out of the water.

3. When the wave is four to five car lengths behind you, start paddling slowly toward shore.

4. When the wave is one car length away (about 16 feet), start paddling as hard as you can.

5. As the wave lifts you up . . .

6. . . . . push yourself to a standing position.

7. Face forward, one leg in front, one in back, knees slightly bent.

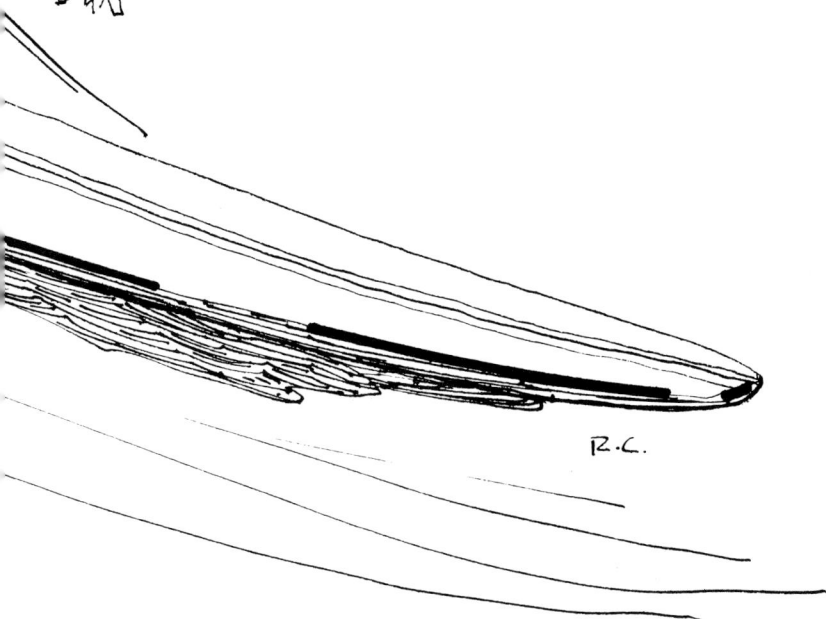

R.C.

Control Your Direction

When you are riding the wave, control left and right turns with your rear foot by pushing your toe or heel down with a slight lean, as if you were making a turn with a bicycle.

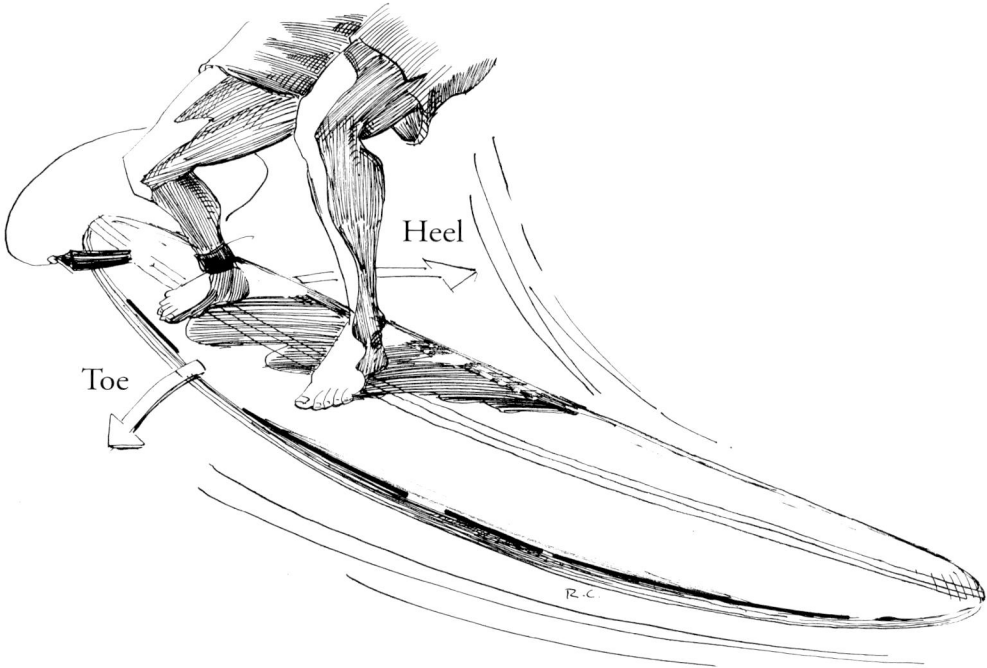

Heel

Toe

Your front foot is used to stabilize the nose and the tail balance. Always look where you are going.

The kind of wave you want to catch depends on whether you are going left, right, or whichever direction the wave is breaking toward. If you try to catch a wave that is straight off the top, there are more chances the wave will close out. Use your discretion.

If the wave has a peak (or point), surf left or right. This is optional at some surf spots. Use your discretion and observe other surfers.

Waves commonly come in sets of two to four.

Possible close out, the wave breaking all at one time

Right break, facing toward the shore

Left break

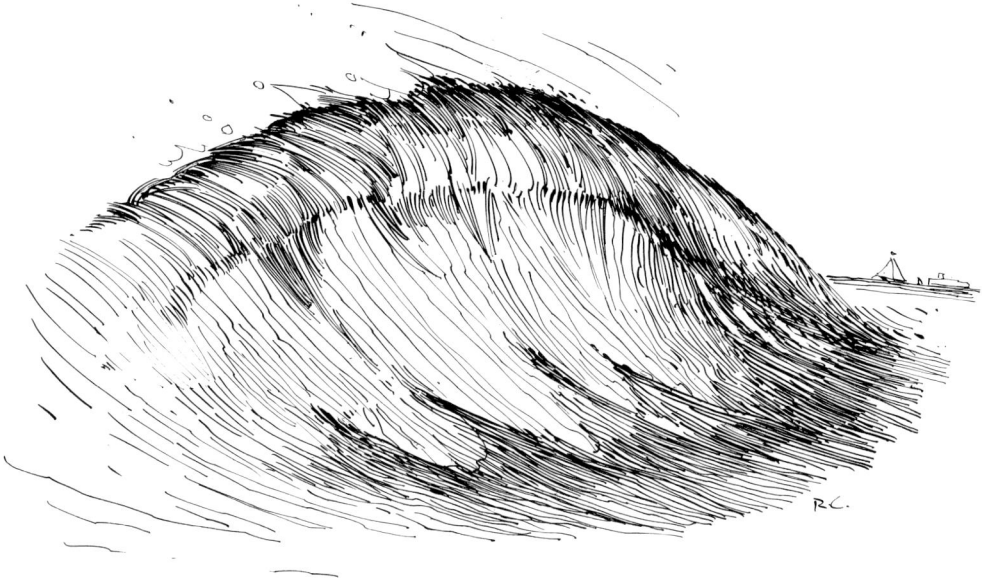

Peak (point)

Wave sets

Pull back out to prevent accidents from occurring and out of common courtesy.

The surfer closest to the break usually
has the right-of-way.

Surfer at this position paddles over the wave or sits and watches with discretion.

Surfer at this position usually sits still or paddles toward the break to avoid collision.

Be prepared to dive!

Surfer coming down.

Surfer at this position must be prepared to dive under the wave to avoid getting hit by the surfboard in front of him.
Try your best to get out of the way. *BE SAFE!*

Bottom Turn

Tube Ride

Off the Lip

Cut Back

Steep Drop

Over the Falls (Wipe Out)

Kick Out (Exit)

Wall (face)

High line

Lip (peel)

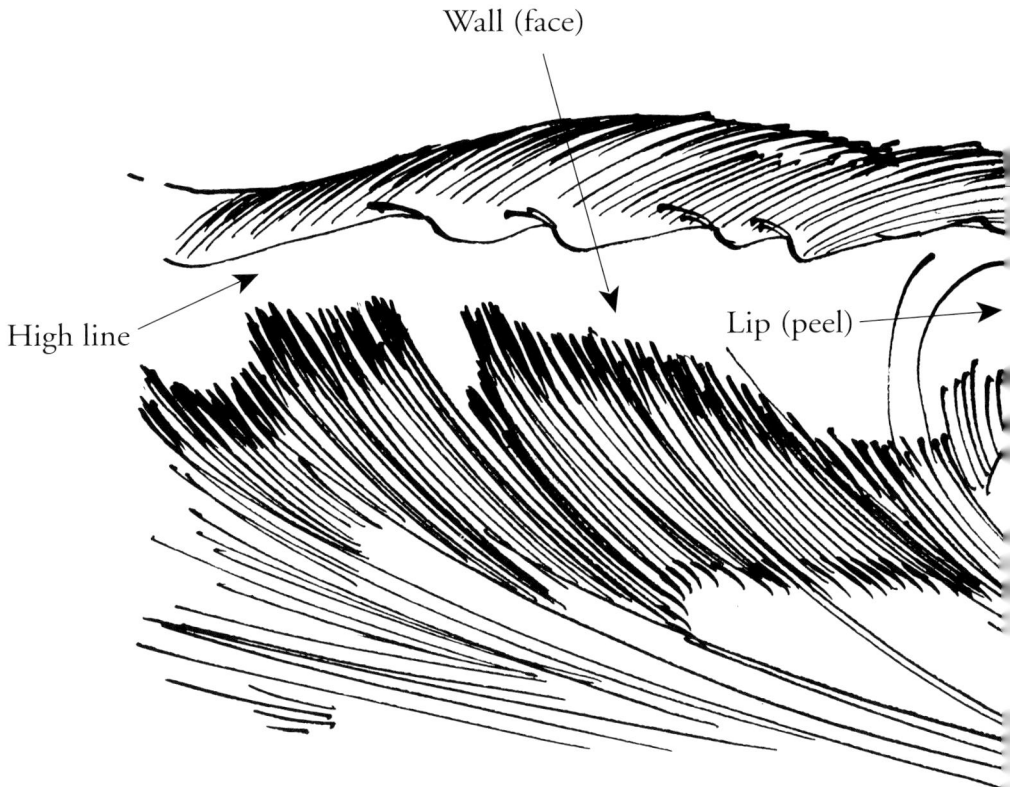

46

Spray

Tube
(pipe)

R.C.

Whitewash

From the Author

I dedicate this book to my wife, Claire, my three children, and all my friends who have supported me on the great challenge of creating this book. I owe special thanks to a dear friend, Donald Stirling, who inspired me to write this guide.

I have been an avid surfer for nearly twenty years, and I have surfed in Guam, California, and Hawai'i. In each place I have found peace and joy in a God-given sanctuary. Since 1997 I have lived in Hawai'i, ever closer to the waves and surf that inspired this book.

I was given formal instruction in the sport of surfing by many experienced surfers and have developed techniques that have helped me surf safely and more efficiently. Over the years I have also taught surfing. It fills my heart to be able to share this simple knowledge with others who strive for the excitement I have found in the sport of surfing. Enjoy!